Hymns of Faith

the words and music
of thirty favorite sacred songs
and the real-life experiences
which prompted their writing

by

Nathanael Olson

An *ideals* Publication

Christianity Is a Singing Faith

If music is "the language of the soul," then sacred music must be the language of the spirit. Who can think of the Christian faith without hearing the sound of singing—Paul and Silas harmonizing in the Philippian jail . . . martyrs singing triumphantly as they march toward the stake . . . slaves creating "spirituals" to ease their minds as they toil under the noonday sun?

Only the Christian faith gives "a song in the night." Atheism has its arguments but no songs. Heathenism has its minor chants but no major melodies. The entertainment world introduces thousands of lyrics and tunes, but few survive the test of time.

Christian hymns are the truly popular songs—living on from generation to generation, bringing hope, comfort and cheer to all who sing them.

Martin Luther, whose hymn, "A Mighty Fortress" has remained popular for over four hundred years, once said, "Music is a fair and glorious gift of God. I would not for the world forego my humble share of music. Singers . . . smile through their troubles in song. Music makes people kinder, gentler . . . and more reasonable . . . The devil flees before the sound of music almost as much as before the Word of God."

For years, the author of this book has made a hobby of discovering and sharing with others the interesting stories behind the hymns we sing. His parents, Peter and Olive Olson, Christian ministers, taught him his first sacred songs and choruses. His wife, Shirley, and their daughters, Melody and Joy, share his love of Gospel music. Therefore, it is of great joy to him to present these findings in beautiful book form.

Naturally, the thirty favorite hymns included are but a representation of the songs Christians sing. Limited space and copyright restrictions have prohibited the inclusion of some.

There are, however, sufficient songs and stories in these eighty pages to inspire reading and singing for many happy hours!

May the Lord bless you as you keep a song in your heart!

Nathanael Olson

ISBN 0-89542-066-X 395

IDEALS PUBLISHING CORP., MILWAUKEE, WIS. 53201
© COPYRIGHT MCMLXXV, PRINTED AND BOUND IN U.S.A.

Music is God's gift to man, the only art of heaven given to earth, the only art of earth we take to heaven.

—*Walter Savage Landor*

He Leadeth Me

"For our study tonight, let us turn to the beloved Twenty-Third Psalm." The voice was that of the Reverend Joseph M. Gilmore, twenty-eight years of age, leading the Wednesday night Bible study at the First Baptist Church in Philadelphia.

During the message, he laid great emphasis on the leading of the Good Shepherd. "He leadeth me beside the still waters..." "He leadeth me in the paths of righteousness."

He told the audience that it is a blessed experience to be led by God. He urged them to follow the Lord as devotedly as sheep follow the shepherd.

After the meeting was dismissed, Gilmore's heart was still pulsating with the thrilling truth of God's leadership. Taking the paper on which his sermon notes were written, he turned the sheets over and began to write. Sometime later, he handed the completed poem to his wife.

She, in turn, without his knowledge, mailed the poem to *The Watchman and Reflector*, a paper published in Boston. When it was published, William Bradbury, the noted composer, saw the poem, liked it, and matched the lovely lines with a melody which has enhanced its beauty.

Somehow, the Reverend Gilmore thought that the chorus of his hymn had been written and added by someone else. However, after his wife's death, he discovered the original manuscript. There, in his own handwriting, was the refrain—proof that he had indeed composed the chorus at the same time as the verses!

The Good Shepherd led Joseph Gilmore all the days of his eighty-four years. Although history records that his father was the Governor of New Hampshire, and that Joseph was successful in both religious and educational circles, the general Christian public remembers him for his poetic reminder that God *is* leading!

4

He Leadeth Me

Joseph H. Gilmore

Wm. B. Bradbury

1. He lead-eth, me O bless-ed tho't! O words with heav'nly comfort fraught!
2. Sometimes 'mid scenes of deepest gloom, Sometimes where Eden's bowers bloom,
3. Lord, I would clasp Thy hand in mine, Nor ev-er mur-mur nor re-pine,
4. And when my task on earth is done, When, by Thy grace, the vic-t'ry's won,

What-e'er I do, wher-e'er I be, Still 'tis God's hand that lead-eth me.
By wa-ters still, o'er trou-bled sea,—Still 'tis His hand that lead-eth me!
Con-tent, what-ev-er lot I see, Since 'tis my God that lead-eth me!
E'en death's cold wave I will not flee, Since God thro' Jor-dan lead-eth me.

REFRAIN

{ He lead-eth me, He lead-eth me! By His own hand He leadeth me!
{ His faithful foll'wer I would be, For by His hand He (*Omit.....*) leadeth me.

How Great Thou Art

"The heavens declare the glory of God and the firmament showeth his handiwork." (Psalm 19:1)

Many poets and songsmiths have expressed their wonder of God's creation, but few have struck such a responsive chord in the hearts of millions as did the writer of this hymn—currently *the* most popular sacred song.

It is, in reality, not a new hymn.

The original poem was penned around 1885 by the Reverend Carl Boberg, a well-known Lutheran minister and editor of his day. (At one time, he served as a senator in the Swedish parliament.)

It is reported that Boberg was inspired to write, "O Store Gud" (O Great God) as he viewed with awe the sparkling beauty of Sweden's lakes and meadows following a summer thunderstorm.

The hymn was translated into other languages such as German and Russian. The version which lifted this hymn to worldwide acceptance, however, was the English translation by Stuart K. Hine.

A copy of these moving words was handed to Mr. George Beverly Shea, soloist for the Billy Graham Crusades. Mr. Shea introduced the hymn at the 1955 Crusade in Toronto, Ontario, Canada. The rest is history! "How Great Thou Art" captured the hearts and minds of hymn lovers everywhere. During the 1957 New York Crusade, Mr. Shea and the Crusade Choir sang this hymn ninety-nine times!

Perhaps the immense popularity of this hymn is due to the fact that man is, by nature, a worshiping creature. When this desire to worship is coupled with moving words and a simple melody, such as "How Great Thou Art" offers, millions take up the wonder the poet felt when he wrote his innermost feelings about his Creator.

Note: The words and music of this copyrighted hymn are available in sheet music from Manna Music, Inc.

God talks to us through His creation.

The heavens and the earth declare His glory.

What A Friend

This beloved poem, written to comfort one person, has brought consolation and help to millions of people the world over. The author, Joseph Scriven, discovered early in life how much he needed the friendship of Christ. Born in 1820 in Dublin, Ireland, he was graduated from that city's Trinity College and looked forward to a happy life with the Irish lass of his choice. But then tragedy struck. On the eve of his wedding, his fiancée was accidentally drowned.

Lonely and unable to continue his training as a military cadet because of poor health, he left the Emerald Isle and came to Port Hope, Ontario, Canada when he was twenty-five years old. He became the local "Good Samaritan"—helping the poor and underprivileged. He often shared his food with the needy and even gave them his clothes. He would work only for those too poor to pay him for his services.

All these good deeds, however, might have been forgotten by Christendom had not Joseph Scriven written twenty-four lines to comfort his mother during a time of serious illness. It had been ten years since he had kissed her goodbye and he was now unable to go back to be with her. So he produced this poem and sent it with the prayer that it would remind her of her never-failing Friend, Christ Jesus.

Scriven's copy of these immortal lines lay dormant in his bedroom until a neighbor found them and asked, "Who wrote these beautiful words?" He modestly replied, "The Lord and I did it between us."

Sometime later these words appeared in a periodical and were eventually seen by a German-American lawyer and composer, Charles Converse, whose simple but plaintive tune gave the wings of melody to Scriven's three verses. Thus an Irish-Canadian and a German-American were used by God to bless untold millions through this favorite sacred song.

Scriven lived and died a socially lonely man. (His second fiancée died after a brief illness.) From the spiritual perspective, however, he was never alone because he knew in a personal way, the Friend "that sticketh closer than a brother." (Proverbs 18:24)

What A Friend

Joseph Scriven   Charles Converse

1. What a Friend we have in Je - sus, All our sins and griefs to bear!
2. Have we tri - als and temp - ta - tions? Is there troub-le an - y - where?
3. Are we weak and heav-y - la - den, Cumbered with a load of care?—

What a priv - i - lege to car - ry Ev - 'ry-thing to God in prayer!
We should nev-er be dis - cour-aged, Take it to the Lord in prayer.
Pre - cious Sav-ior, still our ref - uge,—Take it to the Lord in prayer.

O what peace we oft - en for - feit, O what need-less pain we bear,
Can we find a friend so faith - ful Who will all our sor-rows share?
Do thy friends despise, for-sake thee? Take it to the Lord in prayer;

All be-cause we do not car - ry Ev - 'ry-thing to God in prayer!
Je - sus knows our ev - 'ry weak - ness, Take it to the Lord in prayer.
In His arms He'll take and shield thee, Thou wilt find a sol - ace there.

When I Survey the Wondrous Cross

From a Gregorian Chant
Arr. by Lowell Mason

Isaac Watts

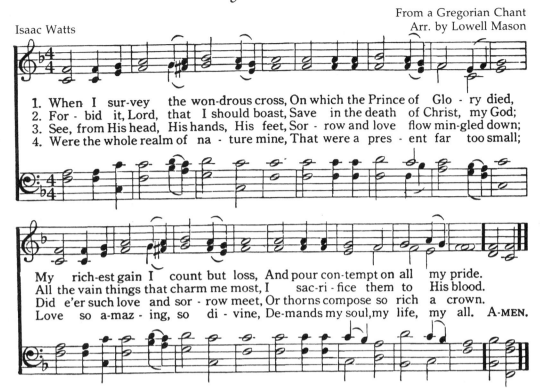

1. When I sur-vey the won-drous cross, On which the Prince of Glo-ry died,
2. For-bid it, Lord, that I should boast, Save in the death of Christ, my God;
3. See, from His head, His hands, His feet, Sor-row and love flow min-gled down;
4. Were the whole realm of na-ture mine, That were a pres-ent far too small;

My rich-est gain I count but loss, And pour con-tempt on all my pride.
All the vain things that charm me most, I sac-ri-fice them to His blood.
Did e'er such love and sor-row meet, Or thorns compose so rich a crown.
Love so a-maz-ing, so di-vine, De-mands my soul, my life, my all. A-MEN.

A generation gap back in the seventeenth century? It seemed that way when teen-age Isaac Watts complained to his father about the monotonous way Christians in England sang the Old Testament Psalms. To him, the singing of God's praise was the form of worship nearest to heaven. And he went on to argue, "Its performance among us is the worst on earth!"

"All right young man," snapped his father, a leading deacon. "Give us something better!"

Isaac accepted the challenge, eventually writing a total of more than six hundred hymns, earning him the title, "father of English hymnody."

Even in childhood, Isaac had shown a passion for poetry, rhyming even everyday conversation. His serious-minded father, after several warnings, decided to spank the rhyming nonsense out of his son. Imagine his chagrin when he heard a tearful Isaac plead,

"O father, do some pity take
And I will no more verses make."

Choirs and congregations rejoice that he did not keep this impromptu promise or else they would not have had the thrill of singing such favorites as, "O God, Our Help in Ages Past," "Am I a Soldier of the Cross?," "Joy to the World" and a host of other hymns bearing the name of Isaac Watts.

"When I Survey" has been called "the very best hymn in the English language." Watts, using only sixteen lines, paints a soul-stirring picture of Jesus Christ's death on the cross coupled with the wholehearted response of the believer to such amazing love.

Blessed Assurance

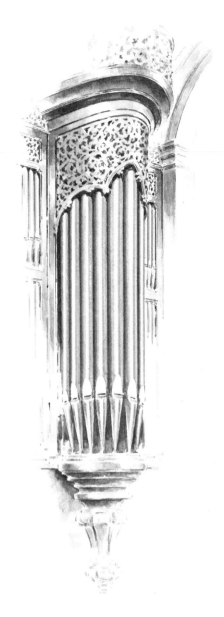

Fanny J. Crosby, the author of this hymn-poem, is the personification of *quality* and *quantity* living. She lived nearly ninety-five years and penned over seven thousand hymns!

Even more remarkable is the fact that she accomplished all this work without the aid of eyesight. Due to improper medical treatment, she became blind when only six weeks old.

At the age of twelve, she entered the New York City School for the Blind. Years later, from 1847 to 1858, she taught at the same school. During this period, she became a good friend of the secretary of the New York School for the Blind. He was later to become President of the United States—Grover Cleveland.

From her prolific pen flowed such beloved hymns as "Near the Cross," "Saved by Grace" and the song, "Blessed Assurance."

The story behind this hymn is fascinating.

One day Fanny Crosby was the guest of Mrs. Joseph F. Knapp, whose husband was one of the founders of the Metropolitan Life Insurance Company. In their palatial home they had a pipe organ installed, believed to be the largest pipe organ ever placed in a private dwelling. Yet on this particular day, Mrs. Knapp called her friend over to the piano, asking her to listen to a new melody she had composed. She played it over three or four times, then asked, "What do you think the tune says?"

"Blessed assurance, Jesus is mine!" Fanny Crosby answered enthusiastically. "Oh, what a foretaste of glory divine!"

In a few minutes a song was born—words by Fanny Crosby and music by Mrs. Joseph Knapp.

Written in 1873, "Blessed Assurance" remains popular among millions of people who know, as did the blind poetess, that "Jesus is mine."

Blessed Assurance

Fanny J. Crosby

Mrs. J. F. Knapp

1. Bless-ed as-sur-ance, Je-sus is mine! Oh, what a fore-taste of
2. Per-fect sub-mis-sion, per-fect de-light, Vi-sions of rap-ture now
3. Per-fect sub-mis-sion, all is at rest, I in my Sav-iour am

glo-ry di-vine! Heir of sal-va-tion, pur-chase of God,
burst on my sight; An-gels de-scend-ing, bring from a-bove
hap-py and blest; Watch-ing and wait-ing, look-ing a-bove,

Born of His Spir-it, washed in His blood.
Ech-oes of mer-cy, whis-pers of love.
Filled with His good-ness, lost in His love.

Chorus

This is my sto-ry, this is my song, Prais-ing my Sav-iour all the day long; This is my sto-ry, this is my song, Prais-ing my Sav-iour all the day long.

Lead, Kindly Light

It has been said that "great songs are born at midnight." If this be true, this beloved old hymn certainly qualifies for greatness. John H. Newman wrote this fervent prayer during one of the darkest hours of his life.

The year was 1833. Newman, emotionally drained from wrestling with conflicting thoughts on religion, had sailed from England to Italy, hoping that rest and a warmer climate would bring him the inner healing he desperately needed. The change of locale, however, brought little, if any, improvement in the young clergyman's condition. Instead, he became ill with fever—and homesickness!

He had to wait three weeks for a ship bound for his homeland—a vessel loaded with a heavy cargo of oranges!

One day, between Corsica and Sardinia, the breeze died and the ship came to a stop. The delay, coupled with the despondency plaguing his mind, caused Newman to go below to his cabin, where, in the stifling heat, he poured out his feelings in a prayer poem:

> "Lead, kindly Light, amid th' encircling gloom,
> Lead Thou me on! The night is dark, and I am far from home;
> Lead Thou me on! . . ."

Thirty years later, John Bacchus Dykes discovered these words in an old magazine. As he hurried along the noisy streets of London, he suddenly "heard" in his mind the melody which lifted Newman's prayer to worldwide popularity. When he reached his study, he harmonized the tune. Another hymn was born! (Dykes also wrote the music for "Holy, Holy, Holy".)

Newman lived to be eighty-nine years old. At the age of seventy-eight, he became a cardinal in the Catholic Church. He is best remembered for the prayer-poem he penned in his thirties when his heart cried out for God to lead his life.

Lead, Kindly Light

John H. Newman

John B. Dykes

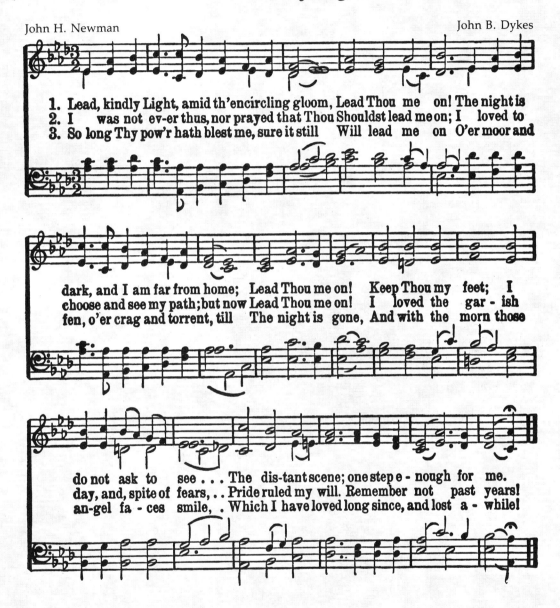

1. Lead, kindly Light, amid th'encircling gloom, Lead Thou me on! The night is
2. I was not ev-er thus, nor prayed that Thou Shouldst lead me on; I loved to
3. So long Thy pow'r hath blest me, sure it still Will lead me on O'er moor and

dark, and I am far from home; Lead Thou me on! Keep Thou my feet; I
choose and see my path; but now Lead Thou me on! I loved the gar - ish
fen, o'er crag and torrent, till The night is gone, And with the morn those

do not ask to see . . . The dis-tant scene; one step e - nough for me.
day, and, spite of fears, . . Pride ruled my will. Remember not past years!
an-gel fa - ces smile, . Which I have loved long since, and lost a - while!

In the Garden

If things had gone as planned, C. Austin Miles would have written only the words to this song. The music would have been by his gifted friend, Dr. Adam Geibel.

One day, Geibel asked Miles to write a hymn-poem, "sympathetic in tone, breathing tenderness in every line." When Miles handed him the requested poem, Geibel tried unsuccessfully to give it an appropriate musical setting. Miles then found additional inspiration to compose a melody which lifted his words to worldwide acceptance.

The words were written in the darkroom where Miles kept his organ and photographic equipment. As he read again the twentieth chapter of John, his favorite Scripture portion, he found himself caught up in the excitement of that moment after the Resurrection when Jesus appeared to Mary Magdalene. Suddenly, his heart throbbed with the wonder Mary must have felt when she realized that the man speaking to her was not *the gardener,* but *her Lord, her Friend*—Victor over death and the grave!

With the creative eye of a photographer and the word power of a poet, C. Austin Miles summed up Mary Magdalene's intense feelings in three verses and a refrain.

Written in 1912, "In the Garden" remains a perennial favorite because it is more than just a reminder of one woman's encounter with Christ. Rather, it is the testimonial song of every reborn Christian who enjoys walking and talking with Christ on a daily basis. Such spiritual relationship is as real in a ghetto as in a garden, on the street as in the sanctuary. The Omnipresent Christ who communed with C. Austin Miles in 1912 still loves to speak to any man, anytime, anywhere. All He needs is someone willing to listen.

The Old Rugged Cross

The year was 1913. The state was Michigan. The minister who kept praying for "a full understanding of the cross and its place in the Christian faith" was the Reverend George Bennard, the man who wrote both the words and the music to "The Old Rugged Cross."

Bennard remembers that his famed song was not born in haste. He prayerfully read everything the Bible had to say about the cross of Christ. He became thoroughly convinced that the cross was more than just a religious symbol—it was the very heart of the Gospel of Jesus, the Lord. Redemption for man comes only through Christ's sacrifice on the cursed tree, the minister concluded.

Gripped by this vision of redemption, the theme of "The Old Rugged Cross" came to him along with the stirring melody. The words, however, were not written until after a two week "test of faith" as Bennard described the waiting period.

Finally, the music and words were wedded into a beautiful union—words of truth on the wings of melody!

The completed song was mailed to Charles H. Gabriel, well-known composer of sacred songs. Gabriel wrote Bennard, "You will hear from this song!"

His prediction was accurate. For many years, "The Old Rugged Cross" was the most popular song in America, either secular or sacred.

Bennard lived forty years after its writing. (The author of this book had the privilege of seeing him in person. He was short, slight of build, with longer than average white hair. A very distinctive gentleman!)

On October 9, 1958, the Reverend George Bennard, age eighty-five, exchanged his cross for a crown. His earthly life had ended, but the music and message God gave him in 1913 lingers on to remind Christians everywhere of the centrality of the cross to the Christian faith.

Note: The words and music of this copyrighted song appear in most hymnals.

Sweet Hour of Prayer

If William Walford of Coleshill, England had not written this hymn-poem, he would have been remembered only as a guest preacher in the churches of that area and as the owner of a small trinket shop. These thirty-two lines multiplied his influence ten thousandfold and made his name remembered one hundred and thirty years after their writing.

It was in 1842 that a friend, Thomas Salmon, a Congregational clergyman, stopped at Walford's shop. This day, instead of the usual showing of his hand-carved ivory trinkets, Walford asked his minister-friend to write down a poem he had just completed:

"Sweet hour of prayer! Sweet hour of prayer!
That calls me from a world of care,
And bids me at my Father's throne
Make all my wants and wishes known.
In seasons of distress and grief,
My soul has often found relief,
And oft escaped the tempter's snare
By thy return, sweet hour of prayer."

Three years later, when Reverend Salmon visited New York City, he showed the old carver's poem to the *New York Observer*. "Sweet Hour of Prayer" appeared in the September, 1845 issue. It was not until fourteen years later, however, that anything dramatic happened to these lovely lines. It was in 1859 that the noted composer, William Bradbury, set Walford's poem to music. Lifted on the wings of melody, this poem on prayer was soon carried around the world and sung by millions who had discovered, as had Walford, that an hour spent in communion with God is truly a *"sweet* hour of prayer."

The reason William Walford asked his friend to write the poem down for him was because he couldn't see how to write. Walford was blind physically, but not spiritually. The eyes of his soul could see perfectly. It took rare insight to create such a meaningful hymn.

Sweet Hour of Prayer

W. W. Walford

Wm. B. Bradbury

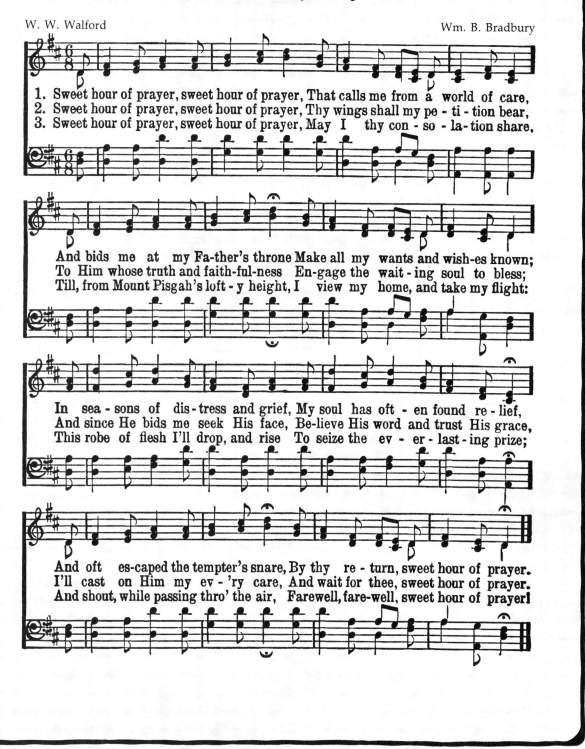

1. Sweet hour of prayer, sweet hour of prayer, That calls me from a world of care,
2. Sweet hour of prayer, sweet hour of prayer, Thy wings shall my pe - ti - tion bear,
3. Sweet hour of prayer, sweet hour of prayer, May I thy con - so - la - tion share,

And bids me at my Fa-ther's throne Make all my wants and wish-es known;
To Him whose truth and faith-ful-ness En-gage the wait-ing soul to bless;
Till, from Mount Pisgah's loft - y height, I view my home, and take my flight:

In sea - sons of dis - tress and grief, My soul has oft - en found re - lief,
And since He bids me seek His face, Be-lieve His word and trust His grace,
This robe of flesh I'll drop, and rise To seize the ev - er - last - ing prize;

And oft es-caped the tempter's snare, By thy re - turn, sweet hour of prayer.
I'll cast on Him my ev - 'ry care, And wait for thee, sweet hour of prayer.
And shout, while passing thro' the air, Farewell, fare-well, sweet hour of prayer!

Abide With Me

It is unfortunate that most people think of this hymn as "a funeral song." While appropriate for funerals, it should be sung in the face of life as well. The author wrote, "In life, in death, O Lord, abide with me."

Henry Francis Lyte, who penned this immortal hymn, sensed the overlapping of time and eternity, life and death. For twenty-four years, he had pastored a seaside church in Lower Brixham, Devonshire, England. His parishioners were husky, seafaring men—a sharp contrast to their beloved pastor who was frail and sickly.

Finally, his health necessitated a change of climate and he was advised to move to the sunny shores of southern Europe. "You have consumption," the medical men told him, "and your only hope of recovery is to soak up all the sun you can."

Reluctantly, he started preparing for the voyage.

In September, 1847, the Sunday before he was to sail, Pastor Lyte asked for the privilege of preaching once more from the old familiar pulpit. His people wondered if he would even have the strength to stand, let alone speak. However, determination rallied his limited energies: "I stand here among you today as alive from the dead, if I may hope to impress it upon you, and induce you to prepare for the solemn hour which must come to all, by a timely acquaintance with the death of Christ."

Later, he served communion to his tearful congregation and closed the service with prayer.

That evening, his anguish found consolation in the lines he wrote:

> *"Abide with me—fast falls the eventide;*
> *The darkness deepens; Lord, with me abide.*
> *When other helpers fail and comforts flee,*
> *Help of the helpless, O abide with me."*

The next day, he sailed for Nice. However, he did not recover. Two months later, on November 20, he uttered the words, "Joy! Peace!" and slipped into eternity.

His spoken ministry was ended but not his written words. Christians everywhere sing them, though nearly one hundred and thirty years have passed since these lines flowed from his pen. The humble heart still desires the abiding presence of Christ.

Abide With Me

H. F. Lyte

W. H. Monk

1. A - bide with me: fast falls the e - ven - tide; The dark - ness
2. Swift to its close ebbs out life's lit - tle day; Earth's joys grow
3. I need Thy pres - ence ev - 'ry pass - ing hour: What but Thy
4. Hold Thou Thy cross be - fore my clos - ing eyes; Shine thro' the

deep - ens; Lord, with me a - bide: When oth - er help - ers fail, and
dim, its glo - ries pass a - way; Change and de - cay in all a -
grace can foil the tempter's pow'r? Who like Thy - self my guide and
gloom, and point me to the skies: Heav'n's morning breaks, and earth's vain

com - forts flee, Help of the help - less, O a - bide with me!
round I see; O Thou who chang - est not, a - bide with me!
stay can be? Thro' cloud and sun - shine, O a - bide with me!
shad - ows flee: In life, in death, O Lord, a - bide with me!

I Need Thee Every Hour

Mrs. Annie S. Hawks

Rev. Robt. Lowry

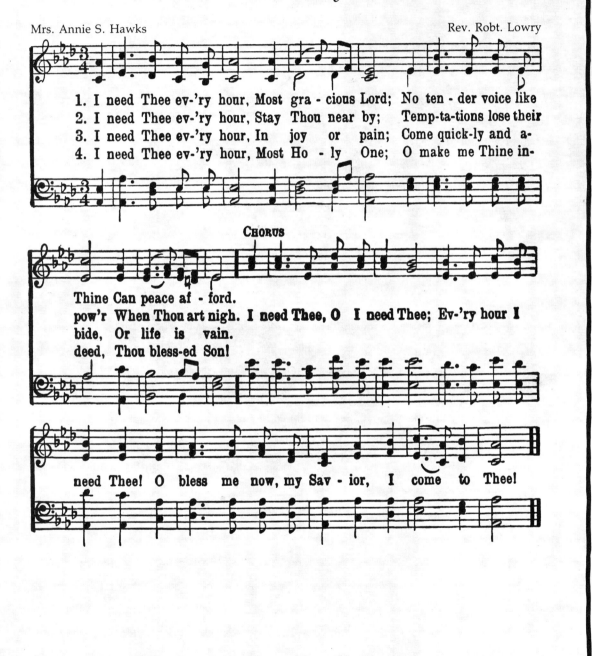

1. I need Thee ev-'ry hour, Most gra-cious Lord; No ten-der voice like
2. I need Thee ev-'ry hour, Stay Thou near by; Temp-ta-tions lose their
3. I need Thee ev-'ry hour, In joy or pain; Come quick-ly and a-
4. I need Thee ev-'ry hour, Most Ho-ly One; O make me Thine in-

Chorus

Thine Can peace af-ford.
pow'r When Thou art nigh. I need Thee, O I need Thee; Ev-'ry hour I
bide, Or life is vain.
deed, Thou bless-ed Son!

need Thee! O bless me now, my Sav-ior, I come to Thee!

I Need Thee
Every Hour

Poetry came as natural as breathing to Annie Sherwood Hawks. She was contributing poems to newspapers when she was only fourteen years of age!

Of the four hundred hymn-poems she wrote in her adult years, only one has survived the test of time. Entitled, "I Need Thee Every Hour," she wrote it rather quickly in the routine of housework. Mrs. Hawks was then thirty-seven years old.

"I remember well the morning, when in the midst of the daily cares of my home," she recalled later, "I was so filled with the sense of the nearness of the Master that, wondering how one could live without Him either in joy or pain, these words, 'I Need Thee Every Hour' were ushered into my mind . . . It was not until long years after, when the shadow fell over my way, that I understood something of the comforting in the words I had been permitted to write . . ."

Mrs. Hawks showed her new prayer-poem to her pastor, Dr. Robert Lowry, the composer of "Shall We Gather At the River," "Up From the Grave He Arose" and other favorites. He immediately saw in Mrs. Hawks' new poem the potential of a prayer-song and composed the melody to which it is sung to this day—over one hundred years later! The song was written in April of 1872.

Perhaps the reason for its perennial popularity is the simple, sincere expression of what every true believer feels—his utter dependence on the Lord for wisdom and strength each hour of every day.

"I need Thee, oh, I need Thee; every hour I need Thee . . ."

Sweet By and By

S. F. Bennett

J. P. Webster

1. There's a land that is fair-er than day, And by faith we can see it a-far; For the Fa-ther waits o-ver the way, To pre-pare us a dwell-ing-place there.

2. We shall sing on that beau-ti-ful shore The mel-o-di-ous songs of the blest, And our spir-its shall sor-row no more, Not a sigh for the bless-ing of rest.

3. To our boun-ti-ful Fa-ther a-bove, We will of-fer our trib-ute of praise, For the glo-ri-ous gift of His love, And the bless-ings that hal-low our days.

CHORUS

In the sweet by and by, We shall meet on that beau-ti-ful shore; In the sweet by and by, We shall meet on that beau-ti-ful shore.

In the sweet by and by, In the sweet by and by,

The Webster House, Elkhorn, Wisconsin

Mr. Webster's piano, music and violin

House interior

Courtesy of the Walworth County Historical Society

Sweet By and By

In Elkhorn, Wisconsin on a quiet winter afternoon, Joseph Webster, violin under his arm, dropped in to see his druggist friend, Samuel Fillimore Bennett.

Noticing Webster's downcast countenance, Bennett asked, "What's making you look so blue?"

There was a pause. Then Webster replied, "Oh, it's not important. It will be all right by and by."

Bennett was reported to say, "It came to me like a flash that this might be an idea for a song." Taking a paper and pen he began to write:

"There's a land that is fairer than day
And by faith we can see it afar . . ."

The other lines and verses quickly followed, coming like a "revelation" according to their author. "It was not I who wrote, but something within me. My hand did the mechanical labor of writing, but it was the voice of my heart . . . of a belief . . . of a hope for the future."

Bennett handed the new poem to Webster; minutes later a lovely, lively melody floated from Webster's violin across the drugstore where they were catching the ears and hearts of those passing by. One of them, R. R. Crosby remarked, "It will be immortal."

His prediction was accurate; "The Sweet By and By," published in 1868, has kept its popularity for well over a century.

Today, hymn lovers enjoy visiting "The Webster House" in Elkhorn, Wisconsin. Here Helen Kluge of the Walworth County Historical Society gives a warm welcome to the authentic nineteenth century home of the composer of this favorite sacred song.

Onward, Christian Soldiers

The old saying, "Necessity is the mother of invention," holds true in the writing of this popular marching hymn.

The author, Sabine Baring-Gould, wrote it for a special occasion, never dreaming it would live on into the twentieth century and be sung by millions of Christians. He said later that he wrote it in a hurry and that some of the rhyme and meter is incorrect. The children for whom he wrote it, however, didn't notice its imperfections. The occasion was Whitmonday in 1895—a special day for school festivals. Children would march from one village to another, proudly displaying crosses and banners.
Baring-Gould, pastor of the Episcopal church in Horbury, Yorkshire, England, felt they should sing as they marched. Not being able to think of any appropriate words, he sat up quite late the night before the march and wrote these lilting lines. The next day, the children sang them enthusiastically to a different tune than the one used today.

The melody we know was written by Sir Arthur S. Sullivan, famed composer of symphonies, oratorios and operettas, including the still popular "Mikado."

Sullivan's rhythmic tune really comes alive when brass bands, such as the Salvation Army Band, capture the spirit of the church triumphant!

For fifty-two years, Sabine Baring-Gould wrote novels at the rate of one each year. He has more titles listed in the British Museum than any other writer of that era. Yet to the general public, his fame rests in the lines he wrote in a hurry to help children enjoy their march from one village to another.

30

Courtesy of The Salvation Army

Onward, Christian Soldiers

Sabine Baring-Gould

Arthur Sullivan

1. On-ward, Christian soldiers, Marching as to war, With the cross of Je - sus
2. At the sign of tri-umph Satan's host doth flee; On, then, Christian sol-diers,
3. Like a might-y ar - my Moves the Church of God; Brothers, we are treading
4. Onward, then, ye peo - ple, Join our happy throng, Blend with ours your voices

Go - ing on be - fore! Christ, the roy-al Mas - ter, Leads a-gainst the foe;
On to vic - to - ry! Hell's foun-da-tions quiv - er At the shout of praise;
Where the saints have trod; We are not di - vid - ed; All one bod - y we,
In the tri-umph song; Glo - ry, laud, and hon - or, Un - to Christ the King:

REFRAIN

For-ward in - to bat - tle, See His ban-ner go!
Brothers, lift your voi - ces, Loud your anthems raise! Onward, Christian sol-diers,
One in hope and doc - trine, One in char - i - ty.
This thro' countless a - ges Men and an-gels sing.

March-ing as to war, With the cross of Je - sus Go-ing on be - fore!

Martin Luther preaching in Wartburg Castle

God is our refuge and our strength.

–Psalm 46

A Mighty Fortress Is Our God

"The devil hates music because he cannot stand gaiety," said Martin Luther. "Satan can smirk but he cannot laugh; he can sneer but he cannot sing."

Because he believed in the power of song, the great reformer spent much time compiling a hymnal suitable for congregational singing. As one writer has noted, Luther translated the Bible into German "so God might speak *directly* to them in His Word" and compiled a hymnal "so they might *directly* answer Him in their songs." Luther wrote thirty-seven hymns. "A Mighty Fortress" is the best known and best loved. It was written in 1529, a climactic year for Luther and his followers. Emperor Charles V seemed determined to suppress this new movement. When the Reichstag assembled in February at Speier, there was a majority vote to reestablish the former religious-economic system in all German principalities. A formal protest was entered by the Lutheran princes, earning the Lutheran movement the name of *Protest-ant*.

During these days of struggle, Luther found greater inner strength by meditating on Psalm Forty-Six especially the words: "God is our refuge and strength." Soon they inspired a song, beginning with the bold declaration: *Ein feste Burg ist unser Gott* —translated in 1852 by Frederick H. Hedge as: "A mighty fortress is our God." The majestic chorale may have been arranged by Luther from an old Gregorian melody.

This hymn became "the Marseillaise of the Reformation." People sang it in the streets. Martyrs chanted its strains as they awaited death. Its first line is proudly engraved on the base of Luther's monument at Wittenberg.

Although written in the sixteenth century, its message is contemporary. Man still needs a fortress, a hiding place. He still needs God!

A Mighty Fortress Is Our God

Martin Luther
Tr. F. H. Hedge

Martin Luther

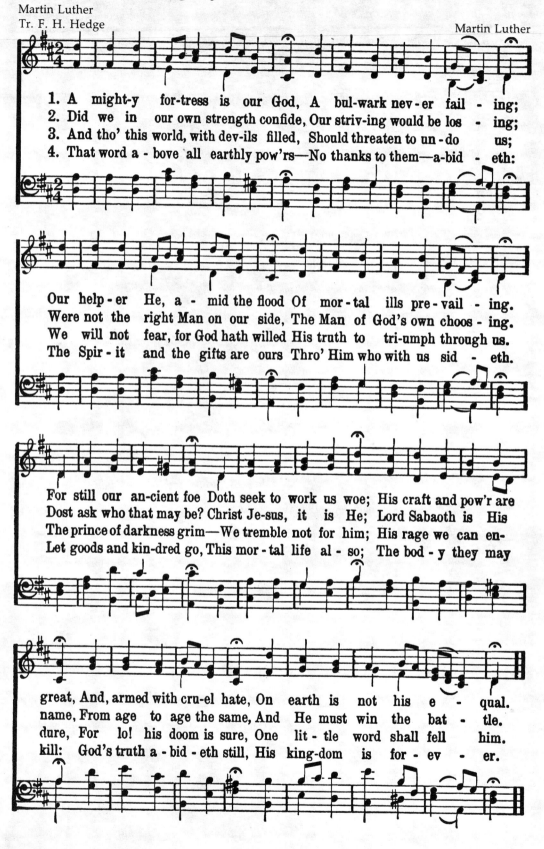

1. A might-y for-tress is our God, A bul-wark nev-er fail - ing;
2. Did we in our own strength confide, Our striv-ing would be los - ing;
3. And tho' this world, with dev-ils filled, Should threaten to un-do us;
4. That word a-bove all earthly pow'rs—No thanks to them—a-bid - eth:

Our help-er He, a - mid the flood Of mor-tal ills pre-vail - ing.
Were not the right Man on our side, The Man of God's own choos - ing.
We will not fear, for God hath willed His truth to tri-umph through us.
The Spir-it and the gifts are ours Thro' Him who with us sid - eth.

For still our an-cient foe Doth seek to work us woe; His craft and pow'r are
Dost ask who that may be? Christ Je-sus, it is He; Lord Sabaoth is His
The prince of darkness grim—We tremble not for him; His rage we can en-
Let goods and kin-dred go, This mor-tal life al-so; The bod-y they may

great, And, armed with cru-el hate, On earth is not his e - qual.
name, From age to age the same, And He must win the bat - tle.
dure, For lo! his doom is sure, One lit-tle word shall fell him.
kill: God's truth a-bid-eth still, His king-dom is for-ev - er.

34

Personal Peace

This contemporary sacred song was born in the heart of its author during the troubled days of 1965 when reports of the Vietnam conflict were flooding the airwaves.

As a young father, he thought of his two daughters: Melody and Joy. A deep concern settled over him. What kind of a world would they face? Could they ever expect a world of peace, a place of security? Had he and his wife, Shirley, been wise in bringing two tender souls into such a world at such a troubled time?

Suddenly, like a burst of sunlight, came the thought: "Personal peace." That was it! He and his wife could teach their daughters how to experience the peace that Jesus gives. No matter how troubled the earth might become, they could still enjoy the peace that Jesus promised: ". . . My peace I give unto you; not as the world giveth give I unto you. Let not your heart be troubled, neither let it be afraid." (John 14:27)

Gripped by this encouraging truth, he penned both the words and music to "Personal Peace." A friend, Jim Bergthold, introduced the song on the *Haven of Rest* broadcast from Hollywood, California, and later made a long-playing record, using "Personal Peace" as the title song.

It has been translated into German by Herbert Apel, a missionary in Austria. He reports that this song finds warm acceptance in the hearts of people who well remember the dark days of World War II.

Ray Redlich has pointed out that "peace is *not* the absence of conflict . . . Rather, it is the total well-being of a person—physical, mental and spiritual . . . a completed and integrated personality."

Who, but "the Prince of Peace," can give such personal peace?

Let the peace of God rule in your hearts.

–Colossians 3:15

A new hymn of faith . . .

Personal Peace

Arr. by Leonard Fox

Nat Olson

1. Peace on earth the an-gels sang so long a - go;___ Have you won-dered can such
2. Soon the Prince of Peace will come to earth a - gain;___ For a thou-sand years of

peace real-ly be so?___ For the world is full of trou-ble; wars nev-er
peace my Lord shall reign;___ Till He comes there'll be no peace on earth I

cease;___ Yet mid it all___ God gives to me His per-son-al peace.
know;___ On-ly the per-son-al peace God prom-ised long a - go.

Chorus:

Per-son-al Peace___ that's what God gives to me___; Per-son-al Peace___ so deep, so

full and free!___ In a world of war and strife, I have peace and I have life;

If you'll be - lieve, you too can re - ceive this Per-son - al Peace___.

Jesus, Lover of My Soul

The day after his conversion to Christ, Charles Wesley wrote his first hymn. From then on, scarcely a day went by that he did not use poetic rhyme and meter to express his deep spiritual feelings.

At one point, he heard the Moravian leader, Peter Bohler exclaim, "Had I a thousand tongues, I would praise Him with all of them." He then used that as the inspiration for his stirring song, "O For a Thousand Tongues to Sing."

Hymn writing came easy to him—anytime, anywhere—in his garden, his study, or on horseback! Christendom still sings such Wesley compositions as, "Love Divine, All Loves Excelling," "Christ the Lord Is Risen Today," "Hark, the Herald Angels Sing" and many others. He wrote a staggering total of six thousand five hundred hymns!

His most popular hymn is "Jesus, Lover of My Soul" written two years after his encounter with Christ as Savior. It is interesting to note that Charles' illustrious brother, John, the founder of Methodism, felt that the word "lover" was too sentimental for a spiritual song and refused to include it in the Methodist hymnal of 1780. In fact, it was never included in a Methodist hymnal until 1797, nine years after Charles' heavenly homegoing!

No one knows for certain what one experience prompted the writing of his favorite hymn. Some have said that a bird flew into Wesley's room for refuge, giving him the idea of flying into the Lord's bosom for protection. Others say a terrible storm at sea motivated him to pen these lines.

Whatever did or did not happen, Charles Wesley wrote a prayer-poem which found a responsive chord in the hearts of tens of thousands.

The music is by an American, Simeon Butler Marsh. The melody came to him while on horseback. He dismounted and jotted down the notes. Thirty years later, his tune and Wesley's words were joined together, and no man has put them asunder!

Jesus, Lover of My Soul

Charles Wesley

S. B. Marsh

1. Je - sus, Lov - er of my soul, Let me to Thy bos - om fly,
2. Oth - er ref - uge have I none; Hangs my help-less soul on Thee.
3. Thou, O Christ, art all I want; More than all in Thee I find.
4. Plen-teous grace with Thee is found, Grace to cov - er all my sin.

While the near - er wa - ters roll, While the tem - pest still is high!
Leave, ah, leave me not a - lone; Still sup-port and com - fort me!
Raise the fall - en, cheer the faint, Heal the sick, and lead the blind.
Let the heal - ing streams a-bound; Make and keep me pure with - in.

Hide me, O my Sav - iour, hide, Till the storm of life is past.
All my trust on Thee is stayed; All my help from Thee I bring.
Just and ho - ly is Thy name; I am all un - righ-teous-ness.
Thou of life the Foun-tain art; Free - ly let me take of Thee.

Safe in - to the ha - ven guide. Oh, re - ceive my soul at last!
Cov - er my de - fense-less head With the shad-ow of Thy wing.
False and full of sin I am; Thou art full of truth and grace.
Spring Thou up with - in my heart; Rise to all e - ter - ni - ty.

Nearer, My God, to Thee

Many poets, including the author of this hymn, have found no better source of inspiration than the Holy Bible, God's Word.

As Sarah Flower Adams read the moving story of Jacob at Bethel (Genesis 28:10-22), a prayer was born in her heart—a yearning to be drawn nearer to the One who had given her the breath of life.

She compiled these lines in November of 1840. Several composers have tried to match melodies with these stirring sentiments. Lowell Mason's "Bethany" has proved to be the most widely accepted. It is an arrangement of an old Irish ballad entitled, "Oft in the Stilly Night."

This union of words and music appeared in 1859.

Sarah Flower inherited her love of words from her father, an editor with a crusading pen. At the age of twenty-nine she was married to an engineer-inventor named William B. Adams. Born in England in 1805, Sarah teamed with her sister, Eliza, in the writing and publishing of sacred songs. "Nearer My God to Thee" appeared in their book, *Hymns and Anthems*, published in 1841.

While caring for her sister, Sarah contracted consumption and passed away at the age of forty-three. Her hymn-poem, however, has lived on for more than one hundred and thirty years!

"Nearer My God to Thee" was the favorite hymn of President William McKinley. As he lay dying, the victim of an assassin's bullet, he was heard to whisper, "Nearer my God to Thee, nearer my God to Thee . . ."

This prayer-song is reported to have been played by the ship's orchestra on the fateful night of April 15, 1912 when the mighty Titanic sank in the icy waters of the Atlantic.

Nearer, My God, to Thee

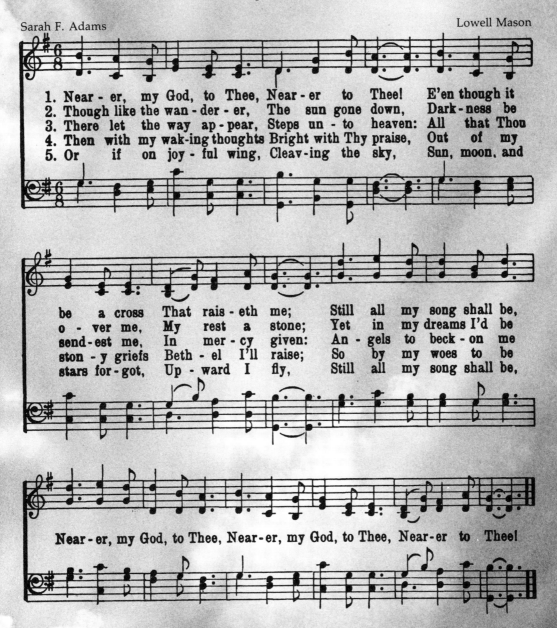

When the Roll Is Called Up Yonder

While walking through an alley not far from his home in Williamsport, Pennsylvania, James M. Black noticed Bessie, teen-age daughter of the local drunkard.

"How would you like to come to our Sunday School?" he asked kindly.

"Sure, I would love to, but . . . " And she glanced sadly at her ragged dress and torn shoes.

"I understand," Mr. Black assured her, and walked on, deep in thought.

The next day, a parcel of new shoes, a dress and a hat arrived at the dilapidated house where Bessie lived. She was overjoyed!

The next time Mr. Black walked by and asked, "Now would you like to come to Sunday School?" she replied enthusiastically, "Oh, yes, indeed!"

During the weeks that followed, Bessie became a faithful member of the Sunday School and also joined the young people's society at the church.

One evening, the roll call at the young people's meeting was being taken. Each young person was to answer by a favorite Scripture verse.

When Bessie's name was called, there was no answer! No one seemed to know why she was not there. All sensed Mr. Black's concern.

He stood to his feet and commented briefly about Bessie's absence, then asked the young people to think about that day when the names are called from the Lamb's Book of Life. "When my name is called up yonder, may I be there to respond!" he said emphatically.

By the time he reached his home, he had formed the first verse. The other two verses followed in just fifteen minutes of time.

Later, he learned that Bessie had been too ill to attend church that night. The illness continued, and in a few days, the teen-age girl went into the presence of the Lord whom she had so recently met in a personal way.

James M. Black found comfort in knowing that when Heaven's roll of the redeemed is called, Bessie would be there to answer sweetly, "Present."

When the Roll Is Called Up Yonder

It Is Well With My Soul

H. G. Spafford

P. P. Bliss

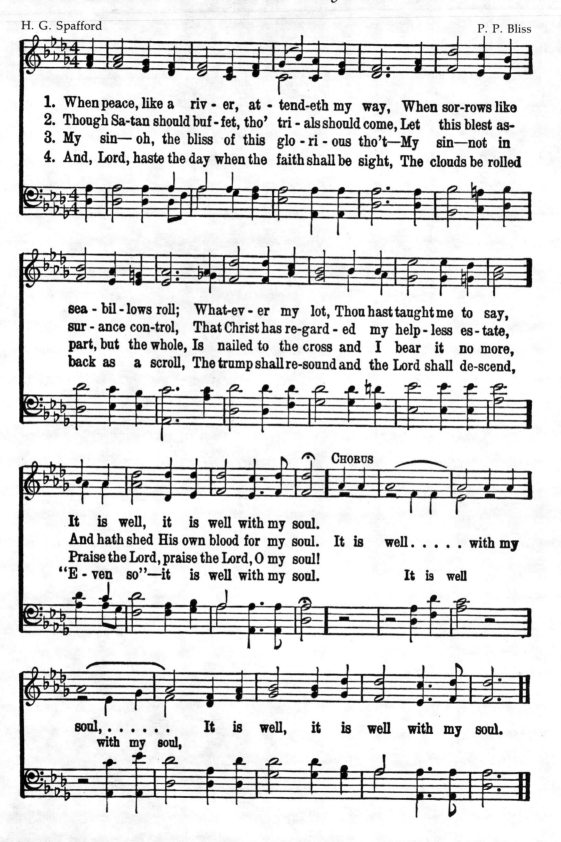

1. When peace, like a riv - er, at - tend-eth my way, When sor-rows like
2. Though Sa-tan should buf - fet, tho' tri - als should come, Let this blest as-
3. My sin— oh, the bliss of this glo - ri - ous tho't—My sin—not in
4. And, Lord, haste the day when the faith shall be sight, The clouds be rolled

sea - bil - lows roll; What-ev - er my lot, Thou hast taught me to say,
sur - ance con-trol, That Christ has re-gard - ed my help - less es - tate,
part, but the whole, Is nailed to the cross and I bear it no more,
back as a scroll, The trump shall re-sound and the Lord shall de-scend,

CHORUS

It is well, it is well with my soul.
And hath shed His own blood for my soul. It is well..... with my
Praise the Lord, praise the Lord, O my soul!
"E - ven so"—it is well with my soul. It is well

soul,...... It is well, it is well with my soul.
with my soul,

It Is Well With My Soul

No premonition of impending danger seemed evident on Mr. H. G. Spafford's face as he kissed his wife and four daughters goodbye when they left Chicago for a visit with relatives in Europe.

He returned to his successful business at home. Some days later, he received a cable from his wife which said, "Saved alone."

He immediately set sail for England to comfort her.

He learned that the French steamer, the *Ville de Havre*, on which his family was traveling, collided in mid-ocean with a large sailing ship. The steamer sank within thirty minutes. Nearly everyone perished. Before the ship sank, however, Mrs. Spafford was able to have prayer with her daughters. She was never to see them again on this earth.

A lifeboat spotted Mrs. Spafford and rescued her. Ten days later, arriving in Cardiff, Wales, she cabled her husband in Chicago.

Evangelist D. L. Moody and his singer, Ira D. Sankey, came from Edinburgh, Scotland to London, England, to comfort their good friends. They found both Mr. and Mrs. Spafford strong in faith, able to say through their tears, "It is well; the will of God be done."

In 1876, three years after the tragedy at sea, Mr. Spafford wrote, "It Is Well With My Soul" in memory of his four precious daughters. He knew they were safe in the arms of Jesus. Each of them had personally received Christ as Savior prior to the fateful voyage.

"Whatever my lot, Thou has taught me to say:
'It is well! It is well with my soul!'"

All Hail the Power

Twenty-three-year-old Edward Perronet was told by John Wesley, the famed Methodist founder, "I want to hear you preach." Perronet replied, "I feel inadequate to preach when you are in the congregation." Finally, Wesley decided to force the young Methodist to preach by announcing him as the morning speaker on the following day.

The next morning, Perronet, resenting this forced assignment, and seeing John Wesley in the audience, announced: "I will deliver the finest and the noblest sermon ever preached!" With that, he began to read the entire Sermon on the Mount! Concluding with the parable of the houses built on the sand and the rock, he brought the service to a close and sat down.

It was to this firey individualist that God entrusted the majestic lines of "All Hail the Power of Jesus' Name." Perronet was past middle age when he wrote these immortal lines. They first appeared in the November, 1779 issue of the *Gospel Magazine* edited by Augustus Toplady, author of "Rock of Ages."

Perronet's poem was matched to a melody entitled "Miles' Lane," composed by William Shrubsole, a twenty-three-year-old organist. Today, "All Hail the Power of Jesus' Name" is generally sung to a tune composed by Oliver Holden of Boston. (The organ on which he composed this melody is on display at Boston's Old South Church.) Holden entitled his composition, "Coronation," after the last line of the poem before him, "And Crown Him Lord of All."

This stirring hymn echoes the thrilling teaching of Philippians 2:9-11: "Wherefore God also hath highly exalted him and given him a name which is above every name: That at the name of Jesus every knee should bow, of things in heaven, and things in earth, and things under the earth; And that every tongue should confess that Jesus Christ is Lord, to the glory of God the Father."

There *is* something wonderful about the name of Jesus.

All Hail the Power

Edward Perronet

Oliver Holden

1. All hail the pow'r of Je - sus' name! Let an - gels pros - trate fall:
2. Ye cho - sen seed of Is - rael's race, Ye ran - somed from the fall,
3. Let ev - 'ry kin - dred, ev - 'ry tribe On this ter - res - trial ball,
4. O that with yon - der sa - cred throng We at His feet may fall!

Bring forth the roy - al di - a - dem, And crown Him Lord of all,
Hail Him who saves you by His grace, And crown Him Lord of all,
To Him all maj - es - ty as - cribe, And crown Him Lord of all,
We'll join the ev - er - last - ing song, And crown Him Lord of all,

Bring forth the roy - al di - a - dem, And crown Him Lord of all!
Hail Him who saves you by His grace, And crown Him Lord of all!
To Him all maj - es - ty as - cribe, And crown Him Lord of all!
We'll join the ev - er - last - ing song, And crown Him Lord of all!

Jesus Loves Me

The year was 1859. Susan and Anna Warner, talented daughters of a New York lawyer, looked proudly at their latest novel, entitled, *Say and Seal* which was soon to become a best seller.

Today, few remember the plot which once stirred the hearts of thousands of readers. It is the simple poem appearing in the novel which lives on and on. "Jesus Loves Me, This I Know"— now over one hundred and ten years old—remains the favorite hymn of children around the world.

Its original setting is interesting.

In *Say and Seal*, two characters, Faith Derrick and John Endecott Linden, show great concern for a very sickly little fellow named Johnny Fax. When his condition becomes critical, he asks Mr. Linden to take him in his arms. The Sunday School teacher picks up the feverish boy and walks slowly back and forth across the room trying to quiet the restless lad.

Suddenly, Johnny says, "Sing."

As Faith listens, she hears Mr. Linden sing a song neither she nor Johnny have ever heard before:

> *"Jesus loves me, this I know,*
> *For the Bible tells me so . . ."*

A few hours later, Johnny Fax's soul went to be with the one who loved him so very much.

The famed composer, William B. Bradbury discovered these lilting lines, set them to music in 1861, and added the chorus which young and old enjoy singing:

> *"Yes, Jesus loves me; Yes, Jesus loves me;*
> *Yes, Jesus loves me; The Bible tells me so."*

My Friend

Jesus Loves Me

Anna B. Warner, alt.

Wm. B. Bradbury

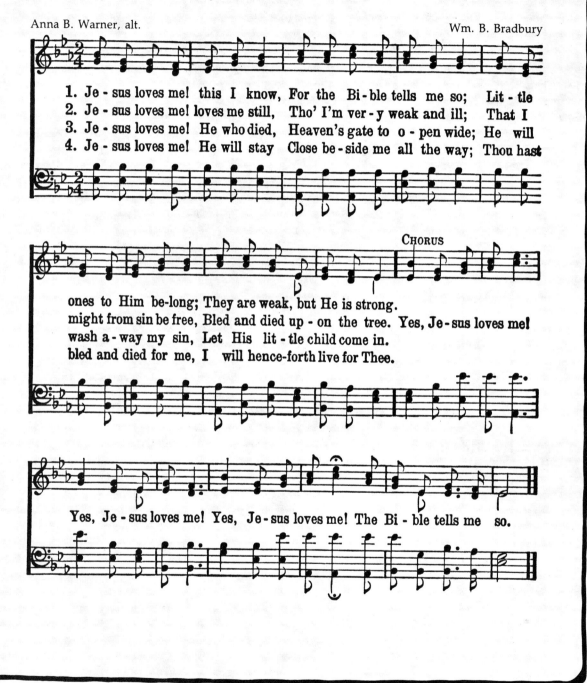

1. Je-sus loves me! this I know, For the Bi-ble tells me so; Lit-tle
2. Je-sus loves me! loves me still, Tho' I'm ver-y weak and ill; That I
3. Je-sus loves me! He who died, Heaven's gate to o-pen wide; He will
4. Je-sus loves me! He will stay Close be-side me all the way; Thou hast

CHORUS

ones to Him be-long; They are weak, but He is strong.
might from sin be free, Bled and died up-on the tree. Yes, Je-sus loves me!
wash a-way my sin, Let His lit-tle child come in.
bled and died for me, I will hence-forth live for Thee.

Yes, Je-sus loves me! Yes, Je-sus loves me! The Bi-ble tells me so.

God Will Take Care of You

Who can comprehend the faith and the wisdom of a child? And how many lives are enriched because a young heart dares to express the voice of God as he hears it?

This beloved hymn, with its assuring message of God's concern and care, might never have come into existence if a minister's son had not expressed a solid logic based on belief in the goodness of our Heavenly Father.

The occasion was a familiar one—illness in the family. The father, a Baptist minister by the name of W. Stillman Martin, was perplexed. He had accepted an invitation to speak at a certain church in New York City. His wife, however, was too ill to accompany him, and he was thinking of canceling his speaking engagement.

Sensing his father's concern, their nine-year-old son asked kindly, "Daddy, don't you think that if God wants you to preach today, He will take care of Mother while you are away?"

The father thought for a moment, then replied, "Yes, son, I know He will."

He kissed his son and wife goodbye and hurried off to minister the Word of God, the Bible.

When he returned sometime later, he was happy to find his wife greatly improved. She handed him a poem which she had written in his absence—a poem of comfort inspired by their son's beautiful faith.

The Reverend Martin placed the poem on the organ, and under the glow of inspiration, he composed a melody which suited his wife's words perfectly.

"Be not dismayed whate'er betide,
God will take care of you . . ."

God Will Take Care of You

C. D. Martin

W. S. Martin

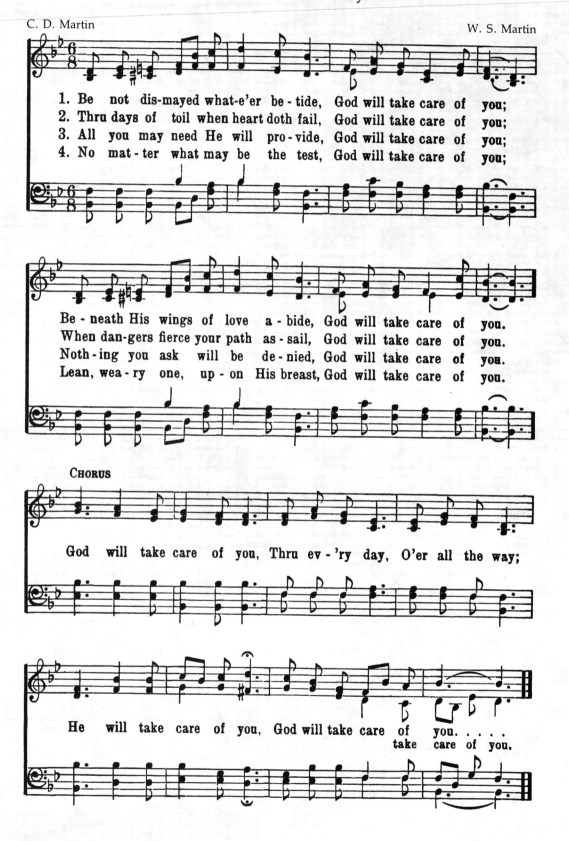

1. Be not dis-mayed what-e'er be-tide, God will take care of you;
2. Thru days of toil when heart doth fail, God will take care of you;
3. All you may need He will pro-vide, God will take care of you;
4. No mat-ter what may be the test, God will take care of you;

Be-neath His wings of love a-bide, God will take care of you.
When dan-gers fierce your path as-sail, God will take care of you.
Noth-ing you ask will be de-nied, God will take care of you.
Lean, wea-ry one, up-on His breast, God will take care of you.

CHORUS

God will take care of you, Thru ev-'ry day, O'er all the way;

He will take care of you, God will take care of you.....
take care of you.

O Love That Wilt Not Let Me Go

This plaintive hymn reveals the spiritual perception a sightless person often has.

Born in Glasgow, Scotland on March 25, 1842, young George Matheson soon sensed the handicap of partial vision. Gradually, the little sight he had diminished and he became engulfed in total darkness. Yet his faith and persistence became stronger. With the help of friends, he took a full course of studies at Glasgow University and became an eloquent minister of the Word of God.

"My blindness has only deepened my dependency on the Lord," he would say triumphantly. His sermons verified this total faith in an All-Wise God.

Matheson possessed a brilliant mind and what is known today as "a photographic memory." His mind photographed sounds rather than sights. After two "readings" of a sermon, he could repeat it perfectly. When he stood in the pulpit, he used an open Bible, even turning the pages from time to time. His presentation was so vivid that visitors who heard him often left the church services unaware of his handicap.

When he was forty-four, St. Bernard's Church in Edinburgh called him to be pastor of its two thousand members. He accepted. He was also invited to come to Balmoral Castle and preach before Queen Victoria.

The most lasting work was his hymn-poem, "O Love That Wilt Not Let Me Go." Concerning its writing he said, "It was the quickest bit of work I ever did in my life. I am quite sure the whole work was completed in five minutes." When these words were wedded to the music of Albert L. Peace, the composer experienced an equally quick flow of inspiration. "The ink of the first note was hardly dry when I composed the tune," he said later.

When Matheson wrote this poem, he was going through what he called "the most severe mental suffering." Although he did not specify what caused the mental anguish, friends reasoned that because the poem poured from his pen on the evening before his sister's wedding, Matheson perhaps was recalling his fiancée in college who refused to marry him, saying bluntly, "I do not want to be the wife of a blind man."

Perhaps it was the memory of that disappointment which prompted him to write of the love that would never let him go.

O Love That Wilt Not Let Me Go

Geo. Matheson

Albert L. Peace

1. O Love that wilt not let me go, I rest my wea - ry
2. O Light that fol - low'st all my way, I yield my flick - 'ring
3. O Joy that seek - est me thro' pain, I can - not close my
4. O Cross that lift - est up my head, I dare not ask to

soul on Thee; I give Thee back the life I owe, That
torch to Thee; My heart re - stores its bor - rowed ray, That
heart to Thee; I trace the rain - bow thro' the rain, And
hide from Thee; I lay in dust life's glo - ry dead, And

in Thine o - cean depths its flow May rich - er, full - er be.
in Thy sun-shine's glow its day May bright-er, fair - er be.
feel the prom - ise is not vain That morn shall tear - less be.
from the ground there blossoms red Life that shall end - less be.

Amazing Grace

The word "grace" has been defined as "God's unmerited favor." John Newton, the author of this poem, would heartily agree with that definition. He knew from personal experience how amazing is the grace of God!

After the death of his mother, when he was only six years old, John took two years of schooling but longed to follow in the steps of his father, a sea captain. At the age of eleven, his dream came true—he was allowed to join his father's ship plying the waters of the Mediterranean.

His dream, however, soon turned into a nightmare. His father rejected him, he clashed with his employers and finally ended up in jail. Released, he continued his immoral living and unrestrained debauchery, working on slave ships for his daily bread.

Then, somehow, Thomas a Kempis' great book, *Imitation of Christ* came into his possession. Through reading this religious masterpiece, his conscience was quickened. Newton, however, did not put his complete faith in Christ until a violent storm at sea almost took his life. When he was thirty-nine, he became a minister and served God and the church faithfully until his death at eighty-two.

During his fifteen-year pastorate at Olney, England, he collaborated with the great poet, William Cowper in the preparation and publication of a hymnal which became popular in Anglican churches.

Of all Newton's songs, "Amazing Grace" remains the favorite. In poetic rhyme and meter he tells the story of his transformation "from blindness to sight," resting his case for the future on the same grace to "lead me home."

In later years he would tell his audiences, "My memory is nearly gone, but I remember two things: that I am a great sinner and that Christ is a great Saviour."

On his tombstone in Olney, England are these words: "John Newton, Clerk; once an infidel and libertine, a servant of slaves in Africa, was by the rich mercy of our Lord and Savior Jesus Christ preserved, restored, pardoned and appointed to preach the faith he had long labored to destroy."

Newton was certainly qualified to describe God's amazing grace!

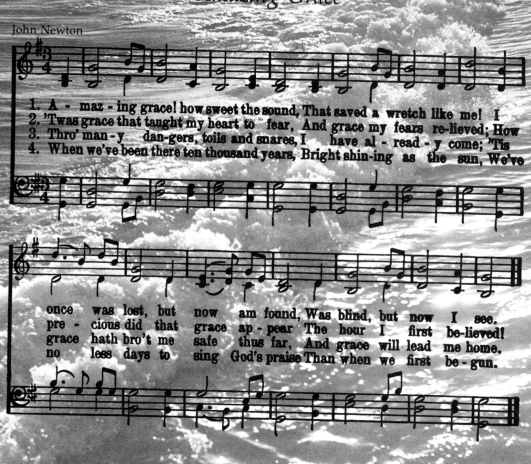

America, the Beautiful

This thirty-two-line tribute to America was born in the heart of a woman whose heredity and vocation had well prepared her to write a word picture of her homeland.

Katharine Lee Bates came from sturdy New England stock. Born in Falmouth, Massachusetts, "down on the Cape" she was justly proud of her rich heritage. She devoted her entire adult life to teaching English at her alma mater, Wellesley College.

During the summer of 1893, Miss Bates took a long trip into the heart of America and there experienced two memorable events which prompted the writing of her immortal poem.

The first event was the wonder she felt as she visited the famed Columbian Exposition, Chicago. There she viewed an "alabaster city"—dazzling, classic beauty of what some felt would be the future cities of America.

The second event which inspired her creative soul was viewing her homeland from Pike's Peak in Colorado. She was overwhelmed by the panorama of Colorado's "purple mountain majesties" and "fruited plain" and the distant "amber waves of grain" of Kansas and Nebraska.

Returning to her hotel room in Colorado Springs, her feelings overflowed into moving verses about her beautiful country with its "spacious skies and shining seas."

But she did not stop with the physical beauties. She sensed the spiritual qualities which had lifted America to greatness and prayed that God would continue to shed His grace on the new world.

Miss Bates did not allow her patriotism to blind her to America's imperfections. "God mend thine every flaw" she wrote.

Today, may we, as Katharine Lee Bates did in 1893, look on America with pride and a prayer. Pride over what has been accomplished; prayer for the wrongs which need to be righted.

. . . for purple mountain majesties

and amber waves of grain . . .

America, the Beautiful

Katherine Lee Bates

Samuel A. Ward

1. O beau - ti - ful for spa-cious skies, For am - ber waves of grain,
2. O beau - ti - ful for pil - grim feet, Whose stern, im-pas-sioned stress
3. O beau - ti - ful for he - roes proved In lib - er - at - ing strife,
4. O beau - ti - ful for pa - triot dream That sees be - yond the years

For pur - ple moun-tain maj - es - ties A - bove the fruit - ed plain!
A thor-ough-fare for free - dom beat A - cross the wil - der - ness!
Who more than self their coun - try loved, And mer - cy more than life!
Thine al - a - bas - ter cit - ies gleam, Undimmed by hu - man tears!

A - mer - i - ca! A - mer - i - ca! God shed His grace on thee,
A - mer - i - ca! A - mer - i - ca! God mend thine ev - 'ry flaw,
A - mer - i - ca! A - mer - i - ca! May God thy gold re - fine,
A - mer - i - ca! A - mer - i - ca! God shed His grace on thee,

And crown thy good with broth - er-hood From sea to shin - ing sea!
Con - firm thy soul in self - con-trol, Thy lib - er - ty in law!
Till all suc-cess be no - ble-ness, And ev - 'ry gain di - vine!
And crown thy good with broth - er-hood From sea to shin - ing sea!

Silent Night, Holy Night

This carol, rated the most popular of all Christmas carols, came into being in a small Austrian town in 1818.

Joseph Mohr, its author, was priest of the Roman Catholic Church of St. Nicholas in Oberndorf, Austria. Franz Grüber, its composer, was the church organist.

A group of touring actors were traveling through the countryside presenting a play based on the Nativity. When they came to Oberndorf, they were shocked to find they could not use the Catholic church because the organ was being repaired. They looked, and sure enough, parts were strewn all over the floor!

"You can meet in our home," one of the townspeople volunteered. So all the interested people, including Father Mohr, went to the home where the play was presented.

The actors portrayed the Nativity with unusual earnestness and feeling. Everyone was deeply moved, especially the priest.

After the play ended, Father Mohr hurried off to meditate high on a hillside overlooking the village. Suddenly, Oberndorf was Bethlehem; the still, clear night of Austria was the holy hush over the hills of Judea. As he walked and contemplated Christ's coming to earth, words took shape in his mind.

> *"Silent night! Holy night!*
> *All is calm, all is bright*
> *Round yon Virgin Mother and Child!*
> *Holy Infant so tender and mild.*
> *Sleep in heavenly peace; sleep in heavenly peace."*

The next morning he handed these lines to Franz Grüber. "See if you can wed these words to a melody," he smiled and said.

A simple, haunting refrain sang itself into the soul of Grüber and he wrote down the notes of what later was called, "Song from Heaven."

When the parishioners gathered for the Christmas Eve service, Mohr and Grüber, accompanied by Grüber's guitar (because the organ still wasn't working), sang for the first time this beloved melody of the holy night when God came to earth in human form.

Over one hundred and fifty years have passed since that Christmas Eve in Oberndorf, but no Christmas anywhere seems complete without the singing of "Silent Night."

Silent Night, Holy Night

Joseph Mohr

Franz Grüber

1. Si - lent night! Ho - ly night! All is calm, all is bright
2. Si - lent night! Ho - ly night! Shep-herds quake at the sight!
3. Si - lent night! Ho - ly night! Son of God, love's pure light

Round yon vir - gin moth-er and Child. Ho - ly In-fant, so ten-der and mild,
Glo - ries stream from heav-en a - far; Heav'n-ly hosts sing, Al - le - lu - ia!
Ra - diant beams from Thy ho-ly face, With the dawn of re - deem - ing grace,

Sleep in heav - en-ly peace, Sleep in heav - en-ly peace.
Christ, the Sav - iour, is born! Christ, the Sav - iour, is born!
Je - sus, Lord, at Thy birth; Je - sus, Lord, at Thy birth.

O Little Town of Bethlehem

Phillips Brooks

Lewis H. Redner

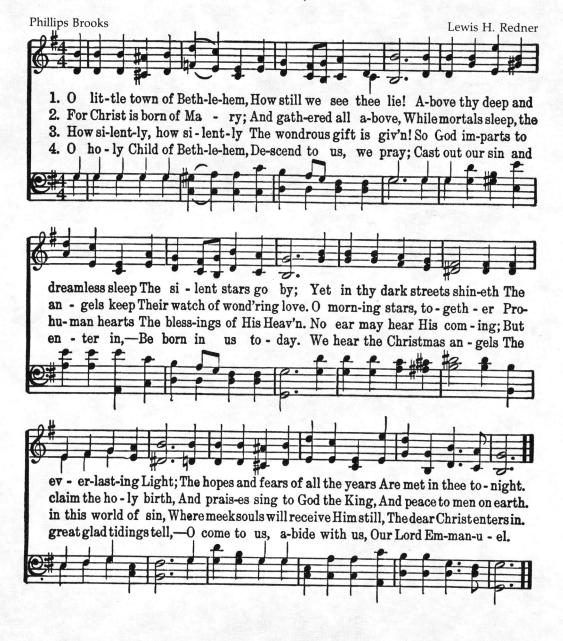

1. O lit-tle town of Beth-le-hem, How still we see thee lie! A-bove thy deep and
2. For Christ is born of Ma - ry; And gath-ered all a-bove, While mortals sleep, the
3. How si-lent-ly, how si-lent-ly The wondrous gift is giv'n! So God im-parts to
4. O ho - ly Child of Beth-le-hem, De-scend to us, we pray; Cast out our sin and

dreamless sleep The si - lent stars go by; Yet in thy dark streets shin-eth The
an - gels keep Their watch of wond'ring love. O morn-ing stars, to - geth - er Pro-
hu-man hearts The bless-ings of His Heav'n. No ear may hear His com - ing; But
en - ter in,—Be born in us to - day. We hear the Christmas an - gels The

ev - er-last-ing Light; The hopes and fears of all the years Are met in thee to - night.
claim the ho - ly birth, And prais-es sing to God the King, And peace to men on earth.
in this world of sin, Where meek souls will receive Him still, The dear Christ enters in.
great glad tidings tell,—O come to us, a-bide with us, Our Lord Em-man-u - el.

O Little Town of Bethlehem

Two men who dearly loved children wrote this carol for some girls and boys to sing on Christmas Day in 1868. Little did they dream then that millions of children *and adults* would sing this beautiful word picture about "the City of David."

The author of this carol, Phillips Brooks, was an Episcopalian bishop and popular pastor of Holy Trinity Church in Philadelphia, Pennsylvania. Well known as a gifted orator and six-foot-six bachelor friend of children, he gladly came down to the level of the younger set—romping with them, laughing at their stories, sharing their smiles and tears.

On a December day in 1868, he decided to do something unusual for the children's Christmas program in his church. He would write his memories of Bethlehem—where he had spent Christmas Eve three years before. Perhaps Lewis Redner, his organist, could match these lines with a melody the children could learn readily.

The Bishop started to write: "O little town of Bethlehem, How still we see thee lie."

Twenty-four lines flowed from his inspired pen. He gave them to Mr. Redner, gifted musician, who not only loved music, but children as well. Through his efforts, the Sunday School of Holy Trinity had mushroomed from thirty-six members to more than one thousand.

Redner liked the words, but could not find the inspiration for an appropriate melody. Then, on the night before Christmas, he stirred from his sleep "as though awakened by an angel strain," as he later described it. Quickly, he jotted down the melody, went back to sleep, and finished harmonizing the new carol in the morning. That same day, he taught the song to the children of Holy Trinity Church. Imagine the joy they had in later years telling their children and grandchildren, "I had the thrill of singing 'O Little Town of Bethlehem' the first time it was ever heard on Christmas Day 1868."

Holy, Holy, Holy

Reginald Heber

John B. Dykes

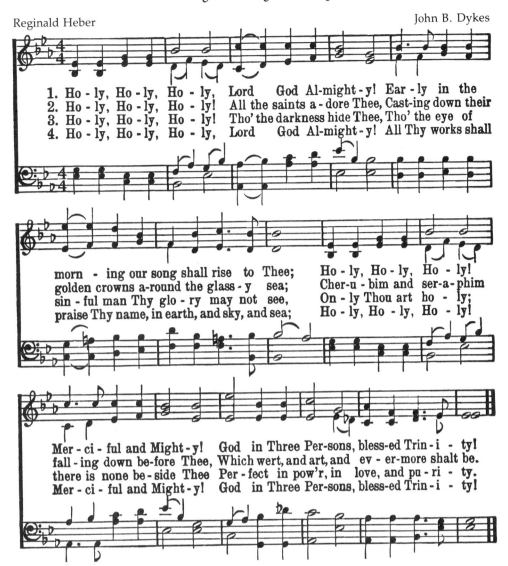

1. Ho-ly, Ho-ly, Ho-ly, Lord God Al-might-y! Ear-ly in the
2. Ho-ly, Ho-ly, Ho-ly! All the saints a-dore Thee, Cast-ing down their
3. Ho-ly, Ho-ly, Ho-ly! Tho' the darkness hide Thee, Tho' the eye of
4. Ho-ly, Ho-ly, Ho-ly, Lord God Al-might-y! All Thy works shall

morn - ing our song shall rise to Thee; Ho-ly, Ho-ly, Ho-ly!
golden crowns a-round the glass-y sea; Cher-u-bim and ser-a-phim
sin-ful man Thy glo-ry may not see, On-ly Thou art ho-ly;
praise Thy name, in earth, and sky, and sea; Ho-ly, Ho-ly, Ho-ly!

Mer-ci-ful and Might-y! God in Three Per-sons, bless-ed Trin-i-ty!
fall-ing down be-fore Thee, Which wert, and art, and ev-er-more shalt be.
there is none be-side Thee Per-fect in pow'r, in love, and pu-ri-ty.
Mer-ci-ful and Might-y! God in Three Per-sons, bless-ed Trin-i-ty!

A man of many talents and ambitions, Reginald Heber once said that his greatest ambition was to improve the hymn singing in the church where he served as vicar—Hodnet, England.

It was during his ministry in Hodnet (1807-1823) that he wrote this hymn-poem to be sung on Trinity Sunday. Perhaps he had in mind Isaiah's vision of ". . . the Lord sitting upon a throne, high and lifted up, and his train filled the temple. Above it stood the seraphims . . . One cried unto another, and said, 'Holy, holy, holy, is the Lord of hosts, the whole earth is full of his glory'." (Isaiah 6:1-3)

The life of Heber reflects the fact that God was more than just a concept to him. Feeling that his Heavenly Father would have him serve on foreign soil, he resigned from his fruitful ministry in England and accepted the post of Bishop of Calcutta. For three years, from 1823 to 1826, he faithfully served the people of the South Pacific. Suddenly, on April 3, 1826, after having preached to a large audience, he went for a swim in a friend's pool, was seized by a stroke, and tragically drowned.

His preaching ministry was over at the early age of forty-three. His poetic tribute to the Trinity, however, lives on and on.

Rock of Ages

One day the Reverend Augustus Montague Toplady was overtaken by a terrible storm as he traveled through Somersetshire, England. He took shelter in a great cleft rock in Burrington Gorge. While waiting for the storm to subside, he penned these immortal lines:

> *"Rock of ages, cleft for me,*
> *Let me hide myself in Thee."*

Sometime later, he used these lines to conclude a potent article he had written for *The Gospel Magazine,* a religious paper of which he was the editor. In this article, he sought to establish the utter sinfulness of man and the necessity of receiving Christ's pardon. To prove his point he compared the sins of the average person to the national debt of England. He had it all figured out that a fifty-year-old man would be guilty of 1,576,800,000 sins!!! Toplady then argued that it was humanly impossible to pay off such a staggering debt against a Holy God. Therefore, man *must* receive Christ "Who hath redeemed us from the curse of the law."

He concluded his article with a "Living and Dying Prayer for the Holiest Believer in the World" which contained the hymn-poem, "Rock of Ages."

Two years after his famed poem was published, Augustus Toplady passed into eternity. He was only thirty-eight years of age!

"Rock of Ages" was a favorite hymn of Queen Victoria and Prince Albert. In his closing moments of life, the Prince was heard to say, "Rock of Ages, cleft for me, let me hide myself in Thee . . ."

Each generation seeks the security that comes from having Jesus Christ as our "hiding place."

Rock of Ages

The Ninety and Nine

In the nineteenth century, the names of Moody and Sankey were as well-known as the names of Billy Graham, Cliff Barrows and George Beverly Shea are today.

D. L. Moody *preached* the Gospel of Christ; Ira D. Sankey *sang* the good news.

One day, in 1874, during their Edinburgh, Scotland Crusade, Sankey discovered a latent talent—composing.

Moody had just finished a stirring sermon on Christ, the Good Shepherd. Turning to his soloist, he whispered, "Can you sing something on this theme?"

Suddenly, Sankey remembered a poem by Elizabeth Clephane which he had clipped out of the newspaper and put in his pocket. "Sing that poem," an inner voice whispered.

Placing the clipping before him, and lifting his heart in prayer for divine assistance, he struck the chord of A flat and began to sing:

"There were ninety and nine that safely lay
in the shelter of the fold,
But one was out on the hills away,
far off from the gates of gold . . ."

The message and melody matched perfectly.

The audience was visibly stirred. When Moody arose to give the invitation, many lost ones responded to the call of Christ.

Ira D. Sankey

Today, this famed organ on which Sankey composed his immortal melody, sits in the chapel at the Billy Graham Evangelistic Association Headquarters in Minneapolis, Minnesota.

Sankey composed many other hymn tunes in the years that followed. But he never forgot the melody God gave him in Edinburgh!

The Ninety and Nine

Elizabeth C. Clephane

Ira D. Sankey

1. There were ninety and nine that safe - ly lay In the shel-ter of the fold,
2. "Lord, Thou hast here Thy ninety and nine; Are they not enough for Thee?"
3. But none of the ransomed ev - er knew How deep were the waters crossed;
4. "Lord, whence are those blood-drops all the way That mark out the mountain's track?"
5. But all thro' the mountains, thunder-riv'n, And up from the rock-y steep,

But one was out on the hills a - way, Far - off from the gates of
But the Shep-herd made answer:"This of Mine Has wan-dered a - way from
Nor how dark was the night that the Lord passed thro' Ere He found His sheep that was
'They were shed for one who had gone a-stray Ere the Shepherd could bring him
There a-rose a glad cry to the gate of heav'n, "Re - joice! I have found My

gold— A - way on the moun - tains wild and bare, A - way from the
Me, And al - tho' the road be rough and steep, I go to the
lost. Out in the des - ert He heard its cry— Sick and
back." "Lord, whence are Thy hands so rent and torn?" "They're pierced to-
sheep!" And the an - gels ech-oed a-round the throne, "Re-joice, for the

ten - der Shepherd's care, A - way from the ten - der Shep-herd's care.
des-ert to find My sheep, I go to the des - ert to find My sheep."
helpless, and ready to die; Sick and helpless, and read-y to die.
night by man-y a thorn; They're pierced to-night by man-y a thorn."
Lord brings back His own! Re - joice, for the Lord brings back His own."

The heart of Julia Ward Howe ached as she watched her beloved nation in the anguish of the Civil War.

She and her husband had come from Boston to Washington, D.C. He was serving as an Army surgeon.

Day after day, as Mrs. Howe watched the troops go by, she heard the strains of "John Brown's Body," a favorite marching song of the men in uniform.

"Why don't you write new words to that tune?" a minister-friend asked her. "I have often prayed that I might," she replied.

Sometime later, the now-famous words rushed into her mind. They came quickly one morning, just before dawn. She hurriedly jotted them down. (The Library of Congress has the original manuscript.)

"Battle Hymn of the Republic" first appeared in the February, 1862 issue of *The Atlantic Monthly*. Soon the nation was singing, "Mine eyes have seen the glory of the coming of the Lord . . ." "Battle Hymn" was destined for immortality!

Battle Hymn
of the Republic

Mine Eyes Have Seen the Glory

Battle Hymn of the Republic

Julia Ward Howe

John Wm. Steffe

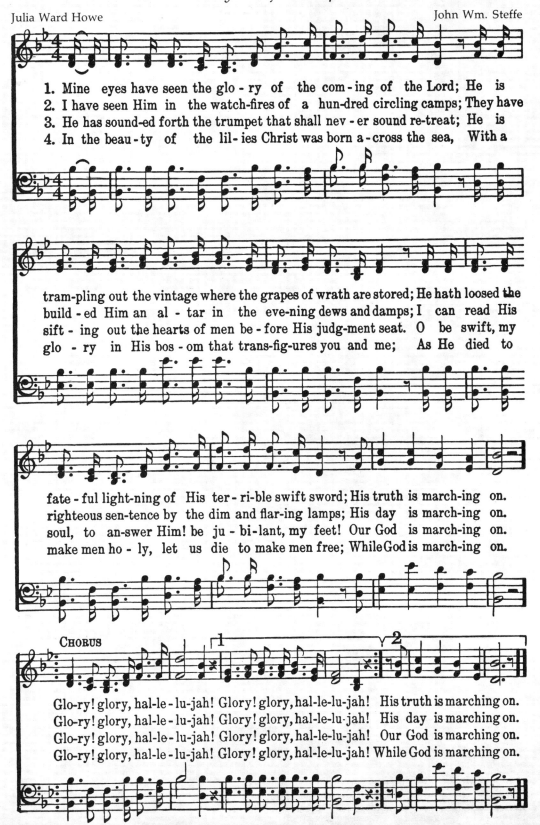

1. Mine eyes have seen the glo-ry of the com-ing of the Lord; He is
2. I have seen Him in the watch-fires of a hun-dred circling camps; They have
3. He has sound-ed forth the trumpet that shall nev-er sound re-treat; He is
4. In the beau-ty of the lil-ies Christ was born a-cross the sea, With a

tram-pling out the vintage where the grapes of wrath are stored; He hath loosed the
build-ed Him an al-tar in the eve-ning dews and damps; I can read His
sift-ing out the hearts of men be-fore His judg-ment seat. O be swift, my
glo-ry in His bos-om that trans-fig-ures you and me; As He died to

fate-ful light-ning of His ter-ri-ble swift sword; His truth is march-ing on.
righteous sen-tence by the dim and flar-ing lamps; His day is march-ing on.
soul, to an-swer Him! be ju-bi-lant, my feet! Our God is march-ing on.
make men ho-ly, let us die to make men free; While God is march-ing on.

CHORUS

Glo-ry! glory, hal-le-lu-jah! Glory! glory, hal-le-lu-jah! His truth is marching on.
Glo-ry! glory, hal-le-lu-jah! Glory! glory, hal-le-lu-jah! His day is marching on.
Glo-ry! glory, hal-le-lu-jah! Glory! glory, hal-le-lu-jah! Our God is marching on.
Glo-ry! glory, hal-le-lu-jah! Glory! glory, hal-le-lu-jah! While God is marching on.

My Faith Looks Up to Thee

My Faith

Looks

Up to Thee

This inspiring hymn-poem was written by a twenty-two-year-old graduate of Yale who never intended anyone else to see his poem.

Ray Palmer, the son of a Rhode Island judge, was in New York City, devoting a year to teaching. One day, during his quiet time with God, his heart was stirred by thoughts of the Lord's great grace and love for him. Deeply conscious of his own needs, he took a loose sheet of paper and began to put his feelings in verse form. He copied the verses into a small book.

A year or two later, while walking down a street in Boston, Palmer met Dr. Lowell Mason, the gifted composer of many hymn tunes. Mason asked his young friend if he had any hymn-poems he would like to contribute to a book that was to be published. Palmer showed him the little notebook he carried. In it was "My Faith Looks Up to Thee."

Dr. Mason showed great interest in the poem and composed the melody, "Olivet" to which it is sung to this day.

Palmer became a Congregational minister and published several books of prose and poetry. Although he lived seventy-eight years, Dr. Mason's prediction made two or three days after he had set Palmer's poem to music surely came true. "Mr. Palmer, you may live many years and do many things, but I think you will be best known to posterity as the author of this song."

"My Faith Looks Up to Thee" has been called "the greatest American hymn." Its simplicity and fervency warm each heart that sings it, bringing the rich grace of God into the problem areas of daily living.

George Beverly Shea, soloist, The Billy Graham Crusades

Just As I Am

Charlotte Elliot

Wm. B. Bradbury

1. Just as I am, with-out one plea, But that Thy blood was shed for me,
2. Just as I am, and wait-ing not To rid my soul of one dark blot,
3. Just as I am, tho' tossed a-bout With many a con-flict, many a doubt,
4. Just as I am, poor, wretched, blind; Sight, riches, heal-ing of the mind,
5. Just as I am, Thou wilt re-ceive, Wilt welcome, pardon, cleanse, relieve;

And that Thou bidd'st me come to Thee, O Lamb of God, I come! I come!
To Thee whose blood can cleanse each spot, O Lamb of God, I come! I come!
Fight-ings and fears with-in, with-out, O Lamb of God, I come! I come!
Yea, all I need, in Thee to find, O Lamb of God, I come! I come!
Be - cause Thy prom-ise I be-lieve, O Lamb of God, I come! I come!

Just As I Am

This beloved hymn-poem might never have been written had not its author, Charlotte Elliott, experienced the bitter emotions of frustration and uselessness.

One day, in her forty-fifth year, Charlotte felt unusually depressed and alone. The members of her family had gone to a pleasant church function. She remained bedridden in her room, as she had been since the age of thirty-two. Before this serious illness came, Charlotte had lived a carefree life, gaining popularity as a portrait artist and writer of humorous verse.

Now all of this past, she felt so useless, so out of the mainstream of life.

Then came nagging doubts about her Christian life. Although she had been a devoted Christian for years, she found herself wondering about her spiritual relationship with Christ. Could she be sure that all was well between her soul and the Savior?

By an act of the will, Charlotte began listing Scriptural reasons for believing that she was truly a child of God. She listed the power of Christ's shed blood; His promise to accept all who would come to Him in faith and repentance; His ability to pardon, to cleanse, and to relieve. They flowed from her pen in poetic rhyme and meter:

> *"Just as I am without one plea*
> *But that Thy blood was shed for me,*
> *And that Thou bidd'st me come to Thee,*
> *O Lamb of God, I come, I come."*

Her prayer-poem came to the attention of the famed American composer, William H. Bradbury. His heart was warmed by the truths expressed by this English lady. He liked the emphasis on claiming Christ's merits, not our own, for finding peace with God. He composed the melody to which these words are sung.

In recent years, "Just As I Am" has been the favorite closing song of the Billy Graham Crusades. George Beverly Shea, backed by the Crusade Choir, sings this prayer-hymn as thousands come to Christ—just as they are!

Charlotte Elliott never regained her health. She was bedridden until her heavenly homegoing at the age of eighty-two. Before her death she received more than one thousand letters from people who thanked her for having written, "Just As I Am." In this way, God proved to her that He can take the one who feels "useless" and make that person truly "useful" to His kingdom!

Keep On Singing!

"Let the saints be joyful in glory: let them sing aloud . . ."

Psalm 149:5

". . . *It is* good to sing praises unto our God . . . Sing unto the Lord with thanksgiving . . ."

Psalm 147:1, 7

". . . Be filled with the Spirit; speaking to yourselves in psalms and hymns and spiritual songs, singing and making melody in your heart to the Lord."

Ephesians 5:18, 19

"And they sing the song of Moses the servant of God, and the song of the Lamb, saying, Great and marvelous *are* thy works, Lord God Almighty . . ."

Revelation 15:3

HYMNS OF FAITH

Index

Designed by
Anise Traynor